MW00959792

Name

Box #

Location

Date

Notes

Name

Box #

Location

Date

Notes

Name

Box #

Location

Date

Notes

Name

Box #

Location

Date

Notes

Name

Box #

Location

Date

Notes

Name

Box #

Location

Date

Notes

Name

Box #

Location

Date

Notes

Name

Box #

Location

Date

Notes

Name

Box #

Location

Date

Notes

Name

Box #

Location

Date

Notes

Name

Box #

Location

Date

Notes

Name

Box #

Location

Date

Notes

Name

Box #

Location

Date

Notes

Name

Box #

Location

Date

Notes

Name

Box #

Location

Date

Notes

Name

Box #

Location

Date

Notes

Name

Box #

Location

Date

Notes

Name

Box #

Location

Date

Notes

Name

Box #

Location

Date

Notes

Name

Box #

Location

Date

Notes

☐ ———————————————————— ☐

☐ ———————————————————— ☐

☐ ———————————————————— ☐

☐ ———————————————————— ☐

☐ ———————————————————— ☐

☐ ———————————————————— ☐

☐ ———————————————————— ☐

☐ ———————————————————— ☐

☐ ———————————————————— ☐

☐ ———————————————————— ☐

Name

Box #

Location

Date

Notes

Name

Box #

Location

Date

Notes

Name

Box #

Location

Date

Notes

Name

Box #

Location

Date

Notes

Name

Box #

Location

Date

Notes

Name

Box #

Location

Date

Notes

Name

Box #

Location

Date

Notes

Name

Box #

Location

Date

Notes

Name

Box #

Location

Date

Notes

Name

Box #

Location

Date

Notes

Name

Box #

Location

Date

Notes

Name

Box #

Location

Date

Notes

Name

Box #

Location

Date

Notes

Name

Box #

Location

Date

Notes

Name

Box #

Location

Date

Notes

Name

Box #

Location

Date

Notes

Name

Box #

Location

Date

Notes

Name

Box #

Location

Date

Notes

Name

Box #

Location

Date

Notes

Name

Box #

Location

Date

Notes

Name

Box #

Location

Date

Notes

Name

Box #

Location

Date

Notes

Name

Box #

Location

Date

Notes

Name

Box #

Location

Date

Notes

Name

Box #

Location

Date

Notes

Name

Box #

Location

Date

Notes

Name

Box #

Location

Date

Notes

- [ ]
- [ ]
- [ ]
- [ ]
- [ ]
- [ ]
- [ ]
- [ ]
- [ ]
- [ ]

Name

Box #

Location

Date

Notes

Name

Box #

Location

Date

Notes

Name

Box #

Location

Date

Notes

Name

Box #

Location

Date

Notes

Name

Box #

Location

Date

Notes

Name

Box #

Location

Date

Notes

Name

Box #

Location

Date

Notes

Name

Box #

Location

Date

Notes

Name

Box #

Location

Date

Notes

Name

Box #

Location

Date

Notes

Name

Box #

Location

Date

Notes

Name

Box #

Location

Date

Notes

Name

Box #

Location

Date

Notes

Name

Box #

Location

Date

Notes

Name

Box #

Location

Date

Notes

Name

Box #

Location

Date

Notes

Name

Box #

Location

Date

Notes

Name

Box #

Location

Date

Notes

Name

Box #

Location

Date

Notes

Name

Box #

Location

Date

Notes

Name

Box #

Location

Date

Notes

Name

Box #

Location

Date

Notes

Name

Box #

Location

Date

Notes

Name

Box #

Location

Date

Notes

Name

Box #

Location

Date

Notes

Name

Box #

Location

Date

Notes

Name

Box #

Location

Date

Notes

Name

Box #

Location

Date

Notes

Name

Box #

Location

Date

Notes

Name

Box #

Location

Date

Notes

Name

Box #

Location

Date

Notes

Name

Box #

Location

Date

Notes

Name

Box #

Location

Date

Notes

Name

Box #

Location

Date

Notes

Name

Box #

Location

Date

Notes

Name

Box #

Location

Date

Notes

Name

Box #

Location

Date

Notes

Name

Box #

Location

Date

Notes

Name

Box #

Location

Date

Notes

Name

Box #

Location

Date

Notes

Name

Box #

Location

Date

Notes

Name

Box #

Location

Date

Notes

Name

Box #

Location

Date

Notes

Name

Box #

Location

Date

Notes

Name

Box #

Location

Date

Notes

Name

Box #

Location

Date

Notes

Name

Box #

Location

Date

Notes

Name

Box #

Location

Date

Notes

Name

Box #

Location

Date

Notes

Name

Box #

Location

Date

Notes

Name

Box #

Location

Date

Notes

Name

Box #

Location

Date

Notes

Name

Box #

Location

Date

Notes